ROLLER COASTERS

FROM CONCEPT TO CONSUMER

BY KEVIN CUNNINGHAM

CHILDREN'S PRESS®

An Imprint of Scholastic Inc.
New York Toronto London Auckland Sydney
Mexico City New Delhi Hong Kong
Danbury, Connecticut

CONTENT CONSULTANT
Korey Kiepert, Engineer and Partner, The Gravity Group

PHOTOGRAPHS © 2014: Alamy Images: 24 (Joshua Sudock/The Orange County Register/ZUMAPRESS.com), 40 (M. Timothy O'Keefe); AP Images: 38 (Brian Branch-Price), 59 (Busch Gardens Tampa), 32 (Craig T. Mathew), 56 (David Duprey), 46 (David Gard), 17 (Disneyland, Paul Hiffmeyer), 5 left, 41 bottom (Dollywood, Steven Bridges), 14 (Gene J. Puskar), 15 bottom (H. Marc Larson, Press-Gazette), 30 (Itsuo Inouye), 13 (Keith Srakocic), 41 top (Kevork Djansezian), 58 (Michael Patrick, Knoxville News Sentinel), 6 (Mike Derer), 47 (Richmond Times-Dispatch, Dean Hoffmeyer), 57 (Sandusky Register, Tim Fleck), 5 right, 51 (Six Flags Great Adventure), 49 (Six Flags Over Georgia), 52 (The Bloomsburg Press Enterprise, Jimmy May), 29 (Tim Larsen); Corbis Images/Bettmann: 9; Dreamstime/Jinfeng Zhang: 25; Getty Images: 4 right, 28 (Debbie Egan-Chin/NY Daily News Archive), 53 (Joe McNally), 44 (Mathew Imaging/WireImage), cover (YOSHIKAZU TSUNO/AFP); Joel A. Rogers/www.CoasterGallery.com: 15 top, 20, 23, 26; Landov: 3, 54 right, 55 bottom (J.W. ALKER/DPA), 27 (JUMANA EL HELOUEH/Reuters); Library of Congress/Detroit Publishing Co. no. 013711/State Historical Society of Colorado, 1949: 16; Michigan's Adventure, Muskegon, MI: 12; Newscom: 34 (Evan Yee/ZUMA Press), 43 (Peter Muller Cultura); Shutterstock, Inc.: 11 top (AndreyBrusov), 10 (IvicaNS), 54 left (Ruslan Kerimov), 55 top (Stephen Coburn), 42 (StockLite); Six Flags Great America & Hurricane Harbor: 4 left, 19, 31, 48; Six Flags Magic Mountain, Valencia, CA: 35; Superstock, Inc./age fotostock: 50; The Art Archive at Art Resource/Kharbine-Tapabor/Coll. Jean Vigne: 8; The Granger Collection/AGIP - Rue des Archives: 11 bottom; The Gravity Group, LLC: 22, 36, 37, 39; Wikipedia/Joekid: 18.

LIBRARY OF CONGRESS CATALOGING-IN-PUBLICATION DATA
Cunningham, Kevin, 1966–
  Roller coasters : from concept to consumer / by Kevin Cunningham.
  p. cm. — (Calling all innovators, A Career for You.)
  Includes bibliographical references and index.
  ISBN 978-0-531-26521-5 (lib. bdg.) — ISBN 978-0-531-22009-2 (pbk.)
  1. Roller coasters — Design and construction — Juvenile literature. 2. Engineering — Vocational guidance — Juvenile literature. 3. Roller coasters — History — Juvenile literature. I. Title.
  GV1860.R64C86 2013
  620.0023 — dc23   2012034320

All rights reserved. Published in 2014 by Children's Press, an imprint of Scholastic Inc.
Printed in the United States of America 113

SCHOLASTIC, CHILDREN'S PRESS, and associated logos are trademarks and/or registered trademarks of Scholastic Inc.

1 2 3 4 5 6 7 8 9 10 R 23 22 21 20 19 18 17 16 15 14

S cience, technology, engineering, arts, and math are the fields that drive innovation. Whether they are finding ways to make our lives easier or developing the latest entertainment, the people who work in these fields are changing the world for the better. Do you have what it takes to join the ranks of today's greatest innovators? Read on to discover whether roller coaster design is a career for you.

TABLE *of* CONTENTS

Batman: The Ride at Six Flags Great America was the first inverted roller coaster.

Kingda Ka is the world's tallest roller coaster.

Some roller coaster cars feature
elaborate shapes and designs.

Artists create images showing what
new roller coasters will look like when
they are completed.

El Toro, a roller coaster at Six Flags Great Adventure in Jackson, New Jersey, drops riders from a peak height of 188 feet (57 meters).

TWISTS, TURNS, LOOPS, AND DROPS

or a brief moment, you can see the entire theme park spread out below you. People look like ants as they wait in long, twisting lines to board brightly colored thrill rides. The rides look like slithering snakes. They curve and bend into incredible shapes, with huge circular loops and hills that rise to dizzying heights. None are quite as high as the ride you are in, though.

Suddenly, your view of the park turns into a blur of color as your coaster drops from its peak. You feel a strange sensation in your stomach as you rapidly **accelerate**. Almost immediately after dropping, you are back near ground level, but not for long. The coaster launches back up from the valley and into one loop, then another, and then one more. As you come out of the final loop and approach the platform where you first boarded, the coaster finally begins to slow down. What a ride!

PAVING THE WAY

1400s	1884	1923	1927
The first flying mountains are created in Russia.	La Marcus Thompson's first roller coaster opens at Coney Island in New York City.	John Miller, Thompson's chief engineer, begins his own coaster company.	Harry G. Traver's Cyclone pushes roller coasters to a thrilling new level.

ON ICE

People have enjoyed roller coasters and other thrill rides for hundreds of years. The basic technology behind roller coasters dates to the 1400s, when Russians passed the long winters hurtling down ice slides on blocks of ice padded with straw. They called these slides flying mountains. These massive rides in the city of St. Petersburg carried passengers the length of several city blocks. As time went on, carved and colorfully painted sleds replaced the ice blocks. Torches burned along the slide's path to allow riding at night.

In 1804, people in France began copying the flying mountains. Covered carriage cars took passengers down what the French called a Russian mountain. Frequent crashes and runaway cars limited the ride's popularity, though huge crowds did show up to watch the wrecks. In 1817, a Russian mountain in Paris may have reached a top speed of 40 miles (64 kilometers) per hour. About 30 years later, **engineers** in France and elsewhere began adding a loop to the rides.

Russian mountains lacked the complex, twisting designs of modern roller coasters.

COMING TO AMERICA

A 19th-century ride called the Mauch Chunk Switchback Railway inspired an inventive American named La Marcus Thompson to enter the thrill ride business. Located in Pennsylvania, the Mauch Chunk Switchback Railway began as a miniature railroad for carrying coal down a mountain, but it soon began to draw thrill-seeking passengers.

Thompson's first roller coaster opened on June 13, 1884, at Coney Island in New York City. For five cents, riders bumped over a few low hills on straight tracks. Customers stood in line for three hours to experience the ride. Thompson became a major innovator in coaster technology, building many new rides and earning around 30 coaster-related **patents**. Throughout his career, he hired the best designers and special effects engineers to enhance his coasters. Riders enjoyed sights such as Egyptian pyramids and reenactments of famous disasters as they made their way along the tracks.

Thanks to designers such as La Marcus Thompson, Coney Island became a popular destination for coaster fans in the early 20th century.

La Marcus Thompson is sometimes called the Father of the Roller Coaster.

FIRST THINGS FIRST

The technology behind railroads played an important role in the development of modern roller coasters.

RIDING THE RAILS

Roller coasters as we know them today would not exist if not for the invention of trains and railroads. Early roller coaster designers such as La Marcus Thompson took their inspiration from the railroads. Thompson even advertised many of his rides as "Scenic Railways" rather than roller coasters.

EARLY INNOVATIONS

The earliest types of railroads were created many years before engines were invented to power trains.

They were simple paved paths that allowed heavy carts to roll more easily across difficult **terrain**. To avoid using more pavement than necessary, the paths were just wide enough for the cartwheels to fit on them. A guiding ridge on either the wheels or the rails kept the carts locked in place as they rolled. These paths first appeared in central Europe during the 16th century and were common in mining areas by the end of the 17th century.

FULL STEAM AHEAD

Inventors first began experimenting with steam-powered engines in the late 17th century. The earliest versions were too large and heavy for practical use, however. It was not until 1803 that English engineer Richard Trevithick built a steam-powered train that ran on tracks. In the following decades, railroads became a common sight throughout many parts of the world, allowing for transportation that was much faster than any previous method. This forever changed the way people traveled and conducted business.

Locomotives forever changed the way people and goods are transported across land.

Trains and roller coasters both have wheels that lock into place on tracks.

TODAY'S TRAINS

Modern trains are no longer powered by simple steam engines. Instead, they rely on electricity or **diesel** fuel to get them from point A to point B. And while they are no longer the world's most dominant form of transportation, trains still play an important role in the way we get around. Every day, trains carry goods and passengers from place to place. Some travel cross-country, while others operate within a single city. Meanwhile, their technological cousins are twisting, dropping, and looping at amusement parks around the world. ✳

UPS AND DOWNS

Traditional roller coasters lack engines. Instead, a cable or chain pulls a train of several cars to the top of a hill. This hill, the coaster's highest point, is known as the lift hill. On the way up, the train builds what scientists and engineers call potential energy.

At the top, the train rolls over the hill and starts downward. Potential energy then becomes kinetic, or moving, energy. Each time the train climbs another hill, some of the kinetic energy is converted back to potential energy. Then the potential energy becomes kinetic energy again on the way down the other side. This process powers the coaster along the tracks until brakes bring passengers to a stop at the end of the ride.

When a ride is close to the ground, it has the most kinetic energy and least amount of potential energy. This means it will be travelling its fastest. Some energy is lost throughout the ride due to **friction**, which is why rides can feel slower toward their end.

The wooden coaster Shivering Timbers, located at Michigan's Adventure in Muskegon, Michigan, builds to a top speed of 57 miles per hour (92 kph) as it drops from the top of its lift hill.

John Miller's Racer coaster has been running at Kennywood in West Mifflin, Pennsylvania, since 1927.

SWEEPING THE NATION

La Marcus Thompson retired in 1915. John Miller, Thompson's chief engineer, went into business for himself in 1923.

Miller and other top designers led the way as roller coaster mania swept the United States in the 1920s. Wooden coasters rose from coast to coast as engineers and designers raced to build longer, faster, and more twist-filled rides. At least 1,500 coasters were in service by the late 1920s. Among the better known was the Racer, designed by Miller, and now a national historic landmark near Pittsburgh, Pennsylvania.

Other inventors jumped into the business as it grew. Edwin Prescott's Loop-the-Loop made Coney Island famous. Crowds loved to watch the coaster go, but few people dared to climb aboard. No coaster matched the grim reputation enjoyed by Harry G. Traver's dreaded Cyclone. Traver built versions of the Cyclone in Ontario, Canada; New Jersey; and Massachusetts. Over the course of a 40-second ride, passengers experienced spiraling dives, steep climbs, a hair-raising figure eight, and sharply banked turns.

PAST MARVELS

MILLER'S MASTERPIECES

After working for the legendary La Marcus Thompson, John Miller helped design roller coasters for the Philadelphia Toboggan Coasters company before striking out on his own. Miller spent his entire life building new coasters and improving the technology behind them. In the process, he became one of the most important innovators in the history of roller coasters, and many of his inventions and designs are still used to build today's top thrill rides.

The Thunderbolt coaster at Kennywood amusement park in West Mifflin, Pennsylvania, was expanded in 1968 from a 1924 John Miller coaster named Pippin.

CLANK, CLANK, CLANK . . .

Many of Miller's inventions specialized in making rides safer. One of his most famous creations is the anti-rollback lever. The device grabbed onto the track if a train car started to fall backward as it moved uphill. The car then stayed locked in place until workers could deal with the problem. A simple device, Miller's anti-rollback lever remains standard equipment on modern roller coasters. The lever also added to the coaster experience in one unexpected way: It provides the now-familiar *clank-clank-clank* sound coasters make as they climb hills. For this and other inventions, Miller was said to be the Thomas Edison of the roller coaster.

LONG-LASTING COASTERS

Over the course of his long career, Miller had a hand in designing more than 130 coasters. Though most have long been closed, a handful of these legendary rides continue to operate today. Jack Rabbit, at the Kennywood amusement park in Pennsylvania, has been running since it opened in 1920. Others, such as the Big Dipper in Aurora, Ohio, have been slightly redesigned and rebuilt in the years since they originally opened. Take a trip to one of Miller's surviving coasters for a chance to experience a piece of thrill ride history! ✳

The Big Dipper in Aurora, Ohio, was named Sky Rocket when Miller designed it in 1925. It operated until 2007.

In 2011, roller coaster designers built a new version of John Miller's famous Zippin Pippin coaster at an amusement park in Green Bay, Wisconsin. Though the original Zippin Pippin had been torn down many years earlier, the designers used old photographs to recreate the ride as closely as possible.

NEW THRILLS

During the second half of the 20th century, designers turned to more daring elements to thrill passengers. One trend was to turn people upside down and then right side up again. Engineers call this looping maneuver an **inversion**. Inversions might look dangerous, but roller coaster engineers make careful calculations to ensure that riders stay pressed into their seats as the coaster goes around a loop. The size and shape of an inversion and the speed of the coaster are all important factors in planning these dazzling loops.

Coaster designers also impress riders by making them feel weightless. As a coaster zooms over the top of a hill, riders feel as if their bodies might float right out of their seats. Roller coaster pros call this feeling **airtime**. Designers space out airtime hills and moments where the riders' bodies are pressed into their seats to give coasters an exciting and unpredictable pace.

JOHN ALLEN

By the beginning of the 1970s, roller coasters had fallen out of fashion. However, designer John Allen's Racer soon renewed the public's love for thrill rides. The Racer was the world's largest wooden coaster when it opened in 1972 at Kings Island in Ohio. After it became a hit, parks everywhere hurried to build their own new roller coasters.

The earliest inversions, such as the one on this coaster in Atlantic City, New Jersey, were built during the late 1800s.

STARTING OUT WITH STEEL

In 1955, animator Walt Disney opened his famous Disneyland theme park in Anaheim, California. Four years later, a new ride called Matterhorn Bobsleds opened at the popular park. The new ride was important in the evolution of roller coaster technology. Built of steel rather than wood, its cars had hard plastic wheels that rolled on tube-shaped steel tracks.

The strength and shape of these new tracks made it easier for engineers to build more stable inversions. A company called Arrow Dynamics used this technology to create a corkscrew-shaped roller coaster in 1975. A New York ride called the Viper went to five inversions in 1982. Today, the Smiler at Alton Towers in Staffordshire, England, holds the record for most inversions. It sends passengers upside down 14 times per ride!

The Matterhorn Bobsleds at Disneyland remain a popular attraction today.

ANTON SCHWARZKOPF

Anton Schwarzkopf began working on roller coasters in the 1950s. In 1964, he completed his first full coaster design, the Wildcat, in Bavaria, Germany. In 1975, Schwarzkopf took inversions to a whole new level with the Great American Revolution at Magic Mountain in Santa Clarita, California. The coasters offered riders a 360-degree loop, a first for steel coasters.

HARNESS SECURES SHOULDERS

ADDITIONAL BAR SECURES WAIST

A unique harness system makes sure riders do not fall out of stand-up coasters such as King Cobra.

STAND UP TALL

Incredible speeds, multiple loops, grand special effects—designers went all out with new designs as steel coasters took the world by storm. In 1984, the Japanese company Togo finished its King Cobra coaster at Kings Island. Unlike any coaster before it, its passengers rode in a standing position.

Stand-up coasters became a major trend in the 1980s and 1990s. The Swiss company Bolliger & Mabillard (B&M), now one of the best-known coaster companies in the world, made its name on stand up coasters. Its first, Iron Wolf, opened in 1990 at Six Flags Great America in Gurnee, Illinois. In 1997, B&M's Chang coaster opened at a Kentucky amusement park. Chang was a stand-up coaster with an incredible five inversions. The first was a record 122 feet (37 meters) high. B&M topped Chang the following year with the unique green steel Riddler's Revenge at California's Six Flags Magic Mountain. It remains the world's fastest and tallest stand-up roller coaster.

TRACKS ON TOP

B&M also broke new ground in 1992, when Batman: The Ride debuted at Six Flags Great America in Gurnee, Illinois. Batman: The Ride opened the era of steel inverted coasters. On these incredible coasters, passengers sit in cars that hang beneath the tracks. This leaves riders' legs dangling outside as the coaster speeds along the track.

Batman: The Ride sent riders through a dizzying 360-degree roll. It became such a huge hit that several new versions opened up in different Six Flags parks over the next several years, and other coaster designers began using the inverted design B&M had pioneered. A daring new roller coaster era had opened. But engineers and designers had even more extreme rides planned for the future.

Today, there are versions of Batman: The Ride at seven different theme parks.

"[Batman: The Ride is] one of the most important events in modern coaster history."
—American Coaster Enthusiasts, an organization of dedicated coaster fans

MANY PEOPLE REMOVE THEIR SHOES WHILE RIDING BATMAN: THE RIDE SO THEY DON'T FALL OFF

Magnum XL-200 was created by coaster designer Ron Toomer.

2

THE LATEST THRILLS

R oller coaster fans define a hypercoaster as a coaster that is more than 200 feet (61 m) tall. The hypercoaster era began in 1989. That year, Magnum XL-200 opened at Cedar Point in Sandusky, Ohio. Standing 205 feet (62 m) tall at its highest point, with a then-record speed of 72 miles per hour (116 kph), Magnum XL-200 gave riders five seconds of airtime during one stretch of its route.

Today's coaster designers are in a constant race to build the tallest, fastest rides possible. Steel Phantom by Arrow Dynamics not only went faster and fell farther than Magnum XL-200, it also had four inversions. The B&M creation Nitro took visitors 230 feet (70 m) into the air inside a dune-buggy-shaped car with no sides. In 1997, the Tower of Terror at Dreamworld in Queensland, Australia, dropped at speeds of 100 miles per hour (161 kph).

It was only the beginning.

TOWERING ABOVE THE REST

2000	2000	2003	2005
Son of Beast becomes the first wooden hypercoaster.	Millennium Force kicks off the era of giga coasters.	Top Thrill Dragster hits a height of 420 feet (128 m).	Kingda Ka takes the title of world's tallest coaster.

WILD WOOD

As rides such as Magnum XL-200 and Steel Phantom brought steel coasters into a new and exciting era, some designers worked to push wooden coasters to new extremes as well. The Voyage, at Holiday World in Indiana, is widely considered one of the greatest wooden coasters in the world. Opened in 2006, this legendary coaster reaches a height of 173 feet (53 m) and plunges riders into a series of five underground tunnels. It also gives passengers a world-record 24.3 seconds of airtime on each ride.

Hades 360, at Mt. Olympus in Wisconsin,

Twister, at Gröna Lund in Stockholm, Sweden, was built using a combination of wood and steel parts.

set a record for the world's longest underground tunnel when it opened in 2005. In 2013, designers added a corkscrew to the ride's tracks, making it the first traditional wooden coaster to go upside down in more than 100 years.

REACHING NEW HEIGHTS

Engineers and designers kept pushing their creations to new heights and speeds. They took advantage of the latest technology while finding ways to go farther with what they already had. In 2000, the first giga coaster appeared. It was called Millennium Force. Giga coasters top the once unthinkable height of 300 feet (91 m). Millennium Force, designed by the Swiss company Intamin for Cedar Point in Sandusky, Ohio, broke the mark by 10 feet (3 m).

The record-breaking coaster used stadium seating. Each row sat a little higher than the one in front of it. This allowed all riders a good view as they dropped from the coaster's lift hill.

Millennium Force was also outfitted with magnetic brakes, a new technology. With magnetic brakes, a metal fin passes between two sets of magnets. This creates a magnetic force that pushes against the fin and slows the train. Magnetic brakes allow for smoother stops. The related increase in safety convinced parks to add the new invention to many older coasters.

Three more giga coasters have been built since Millennium Force. The latest, Leviathan, opened in May 2012 at Canada's Wonderland in Vaughan, Ontario.

Up to 1,300 people can ride Millennium Force every hour.

300-FOOT (91 M) DROP

LIFT HILL

23

FROM THIS TO THAT

THE STRENGTH OF STEEL

Few innovations have changed roller coasters as much as steel tracks. Since their introduction, these tracks have become the most common type used in coaster construction and allow designers to create rides unlike any seen before.

The tracks of the Matterhorn Bobsleds weave in and out of a specially built mountain.

THE MIGHTY MATTERHORN

Though relatively simple by today's standards, the Matterhorn Bobsleds at Disneyland was the first roller coaster ever to use tube-shaped steel tracks. Featuring two tracks that wind alongside each other, the coaster reaches a maximum height of 80 feet (24 m) as its cars weave in and out of a large artificial mountain. The legendary ride is still active today.

Steel tubing has allowed engineers to create the twisting, turning rides that draw crowds to theme parks today.

SHAPING UP

One of the greatest benefits of steel tubing is that it can easily be bent and curved into almost any shape a roller coaster engineer can imagine. This allows for twisting thrill rides such as the Smiler at England's Alton Towers. The Smiler has 14 inversions, more than any other coaster currently operating.

TOWERING ABOVE THE COMPETITION

Because of its strength, steel also allowed engineers to build taller coasters than was previously possible. Many of the tallest coasters today would be extremely difficult to build out of wood. The tallest wooden coaster in operation today is 197 feet (60 m) tall, while the tallest steel coaster is more than twice that height! ✳

PUSHING IT TO THE LIMIT

In 2003, the designers at Intamin celebrated the opening of a new ride that pushed coaster technology into a new era. Top Thrill Dragster, located at Cedar Point, rises to a height of 420 feet (128 m). This incredible height allows the coaster to travel at mind-blowing speeds. Top Thrill Dragster accelerates its passengers from 0 to 120 miles per hour (193 kph) in just four seconds. This made it the fastest and tallest coaster in the world at the time.

Computers are used to control Top Thrill Dragster's speed as it makes a 90-degree climb to its peak. Throughout the ride, the computer adjusts the train's speed to account for wind and other factors that might slow the train.

90-DEGREE CLIMB

TWISTING DROP

Top Thrill Dragster's tracks twist in a spiral as riders drop from the coaster's peak.

Formula Rossa can hold up to 16 riders per trip.

SPECTACULAR SPEEDS

While Top Thrill Dragster is still one of the fastest coasters around, it isn't the king anymore. That title belongs to the incredible Formula Rossa at Ferrari World Abu Dhabi in the United Arab Emirates. Formula Rossa opened to the public in 2010. Like Top Thrill Dragster, it was a creation from the designers at Intamin. The coaster's shape and speed are designed to replicate the experience of riding in a Ferrari Formula One race car. Its speedy trains accelerate from 0 to 149 miles per hour (240 kph) in just four seconds. Because the coaster moves so fast and is located in a sandy desert, passengers are required to wear safety glasses in order to avoid damaging their eyes.

THE KING OF COASTERS

In 2005, a new roller coaster king was born. Kingda Ka, located at Six Flags Great Adventure in Jackson, New Jersey, drew attention from coaster fans around the world. At a maximum height of 456 feet (139 m), it is the tallest roller coaster ever built. And though Formula Rossa has since surpassed it, Kingda Ka was also the fastest coaster in the world when it first opened. It rockets passengers from 0 to 128 miles per hour (206 kph) in 3.5 seconds.

POWERFUL PUMPS

Unlike more traditional coasters, Kingda Ka does not rely on lift chains and gravity to help it speed along the track. Instead, it uses a **hydraulic** pump system to launch its cars forward and up the lift hill. A hydraulic pump applies pressure to liquid in order to generate power. The pump has two spaces divided by a moving part called a piston. Fluid collects in one space. Nitrogen, a gas, collects in the other. The fluid pushes the piston into the nitrogen, a process called compression. Pressure builds. When it is released, the nitrogen forces the hydraulic fluid into a power-generating device called a turbine. The power generated by the turbine then launches the train forward at an incredible speed. Roller coaster pump systems vary in size. Slower coasters might use only one pump. Kingda Ka needs seven.

Up to 18 passengers can ride in each of Kingda Ka's four trains.

THE RIDE OF A LIFETIME

When you first board Kingda Ka, you are strapped securely into one of its four trains of sit-down cars. As the ride begins, the coaster's hydraulic pump system launches you forward at a tremendous speed. Suddenly, the coaster turns 90 degrees upward for a completely **vertical** climb 45 stories into the air. After reaching the peak, you drop down the other side of the hill, which is a 270-degree corkscrew pointing straight at the ground. As you reach the bottom, the coaster begins climbing one more time. The second hill is 129 feet (39 m) tall. This might seem short compared to the coaster's peak, but it is still high in the sky. After coming down the back side of the second hill, your car glides back into the station. Though the ride was only 28 seconds long, you will never forget it! ☀

At peak times, 1,400 people can ride Kingda Ka in a single hour.

Dodonpa's four trains are decorated as a cheetah, a snake, a zebra, and a strawberry.

POWERED BY AIR

In 2001, the engineers at S&S Worldwide introduced Hypersonic XLC, the world's first **pneumatic** roller coaster. S&S took its pneumatic design even farther later that same year with the Dodonpa coaster at Japan's Fuji-Q Highland. Dodonpa blasts riders to 107 miles per hour (172 kph) in 1.8 seconds. Even sports cars and racing motorcycles cannot reach those speeds so quickly. One of the coaster's trademark features is the occasional false failure to launch, complete with loud alarm bells. Just as disappointed riders begin to relax, the train suddenly shoots out of the station.

Another well-known pneumatic coaster is Powder Keg, at Silver Dollar City in Branson, Missouri. This coaster uses a blast of compressed air to rocket passengers from 0 to 53 miles per hour (85 kph) in 2.8 seconds, launching them up the lift hill for a 110-foot (34 m) drop.

THE FEELING OF FLIGHT

Engineers have created rides that let people feel what it's like to soar through the air like a bird. Opened in 2000 and designed by the Dutch company Vekoma, Stealth invited riders into seats that faced the back of the train car. As the train moved out, the seats lowered until the riders were on their backs. The track then turned to put riders face down—the classic flying position. Not surprisingly, flying coasters require extra safety features. A shoulder harness straps in a rider's upper body by pressing pads against the chest. Restraints also secure the midsection and legs.

Not to be outdone, B&M came up with its own flyers. Air and Superman: Ultimate Flight both premiered in 2002. Ultimate Flight allows riders to act like the Man of Steel as they are hurled down the tracks headfirst. It also sends riders through a twisting "pretzel" loop. The pretzel has riders facing the ground and the sky at different points and includes scream-inducing face-first dives.

RIDERS FACE AWAY FROM TRACKS

Superman: Ultimate Flight takes riders through twists and turns that make them feel like they are flying.

Roller coasters might seem dangerous, but they are carefully planned and tested to ensure riders' safety.

CHAPTER THREE

ENGINEERING EXCITEMENT

P art of the experience of riding a roller coaster is feeling a wide range of forces acting on your body. As you speed along a straight path, you feel yourself pressed against the back of your seat. When you drop down a steep incline, your stomach drops and you feel weightless for a few moments. Every detail of a ride is painstakingly plotted out by a team of designers and engineers. The plans made by these designers and engineers make riding a coaster fun, but they are also what keep you safely in your seat.

Roller coasters are extremely complicated machines. Even the smallest details of a coaster design can have a major impact on the experience passengers will have. One small mistake could result in a ride that is unpleasant or even unsafe. From taking measurements to selecting building materials, the designers and engineers at roller coaster companies must work together to carefully plan each new ride.

LANDMARK AMUSEMENT PARKS

1870	1897	1955	1961
Cedar Point opens in Sandusky, Ohio.	Steeplechase Park opens at Coney Island in New York City.	Disneyland opens in Anaheim, California.	Six Flags Over Texas opens in Arlington, Texas.

Taking courses in math and physics in high school is a great way to prepare for a career in roller coaster design.

RUNNING THE NUMBERS

Coasters are too large, complicated, and expensive to be built using trial and error. Roller coaster creators need to be sure of their designs before they ever start building. One way they do this is by putting their math and physics knowledge to use. Coaster designers calculate exactly how fast a train needs to be moving to make it around a loop or up a hill. They can determine how much force will be placed on a passenger's body as the coaster makes a hard, banking turn or spins along a corkscrew inversion.

Computer software can also help roller coaster designers with their plans. Many coaster companies create their own customized programs for designing rides. This software is programmed to make calculations automatically as designers make adjustments to a coaster plan.

LEARNING TO BUILD

People who want to become roller coaster designers cannot simply enroll in college and begin studying thrill rides. While some schools offer a course or two covering coaster design, none offer a full degree program. Instead, future coaster designers almost always major in engineering.

There are many different types of engineering. Some coaster designers specialize in civil engineering. Civil engineers plan and supervise the construction of large structures, from tunnels and bridges to airports and large buildings. Many of the skills required for these projects are also necessary for building roller coasters and other thrill rides.

Coasters such as X2 at Six Flags Magic Mountain are designed by creative, hardworking engineers.

AN INTERVIEW WITH ROLLER COASTER ENGINEER KOREY KIEPERT

Korey Kiepert is an engineer and partner at the Gravity Group, a company that specializes in creating wooden roller coasters. Many of their creations are ranked among the greatest wooden coasters in the world.

When did you start thinking you wanted to be an engineer? Did any person or event inspire that career choice? I always liked tinkering with things. When I was young, I always enjoyed taking things apart to see how they worked. I remember my parents giving me broken appliances (like a can opener) to take apart and explore.

What kinds of classes should a would-be roller coaster designer look to take in middle school, high school, and beyond? In middle school and high school, English class, physics (science), math, drafting/computer-aided design, and typing are important classes.

In college, I studied engineering. To design a ride, civil and mechanical engineering are two good disciplines of study.

What other projects and jobs did you do in school and your work life before the opportunity to design roller coasters came along? How did that work prepare you? I grew up playing with Lego bricks and a Darda racetrack. With the Legos I could build anything, and with the Darda racetrack I could build tracks with loops and anything imaginable.

I was also heavily involved in the Detroit Science & Engineering Fair growing up. In high school, I was a grand award winner multiple times and had the opportunity to compete at the International Science & Engineering Fair.

Do you have a particular project that you're especially proud of, or that you think really took your

Twister at Gröna Lund in Stockholm, Sweden, is one of the many coasters Korey Kiepert has helped work on as part of the Gravity Group.

work to another level? How did you feel going into it and during the process? I'm really proud of Twister. It defines the skyline of the park across the waterways of Stockholm. We fit the ride into an impossible space. The ride interacts with three other roller coasters—going over and under them. It is also comes very close to a flying carpet ride. The park had to remove a coffee stand and two children's rides. We gave them the ride and space for three food stands.

It takes an entire team to design and build a roller coaster. Does working as part of a team come naturally to you, or was it something you had to learn and work on? It varies. Sometimes working with a team is natural, and other times I like to lock myself away and just do my job without any interruptions. I think that I work best as part of a team when there are tight deadlines and I know that it cannot be done without working together like a well-oiled machine.

Let's say someone gave you whatever you need to build your ultimate roller coaster. What would it do? To me, the ultimate roller coaster has a lot more to do with location than it does size. I think that the best roller coaster in the world would be about 3,000 feet (900 m) long and then set in a unique location—maybe hilly terrain deep in the woods or on the water. The ride would have a traditional lift hill. There would be the "click, click, click" as the ride climbed the lift hill. Then at the top guests would be given a glimpse of their surroundings.

What advice would you give to a young person who wants to design and build coasters one day? I would recommend writing letters to the different companies that design rides. If engineers have time, they will generally try to write a note back. I had some encouraging letters (and some discouraging letters) written back to me. Ultimately, don't give up on your dreams. I didn't give up, and as a result I've been able to work on some amazing rides. ✴

TRACKS ASSEMBLED IN SECTIONS ↗

A single piece of the Kingda Ka track weighs around 9,000 pounds (4,000 kilograms). Structural engineers must ensure that such incredibly heavy objects are supported properly and will not collapse.

MECHANICAL MINDS

Many roller coaster designers learn about structural engineering. Structural engineers are able to determine whether structures will be able to support the necessary amount of weight and hold up over time. They figure out what kinds of materials and construction methods need to be used to make a sturdy, useful structure.

Most roller coaster designers specialize in mechanical engineering. They use math and physics to plan out the dynamics of a coaster. For example, they might calculate the speed a coaster needs to be moving in order to make it all the way around an inversion of a certain size and shape. They would also calculate the forces that this movement would exert upon the rider, the coaster cars, and the tracks.

IT'S ELECTRIC!

Electrical engineering also plays a role in the creation of modern coasters. Most of today's coasters rely on electronics and computers to propel them, keep them safe, and add special effects to the experience. Electrical engineers design and test the components that make up these advanced systems, whether it is an electronic brake that keeps the coaster from going too fast or a hologram projector that adds atmosphere to the beginning of the ride. They determine what parts the systems will require and find ways to power them.

Electrical systems such as this coaster operation panel are designed and tested by electrical engineers.

THE ARTISTIC SIDE

Dragon Challenge at Universal Studios Islands of Adventure in Orlando, Florida, uses red and blue dragons to represent its two interweaving tracks.

MORE THAN JUST A RIDE

Modern theme parks often rely on more than just plain roller coasters to draw in customers. Many of today's most popular thrill rides incorporate atmospheric themes that provide passengers with a rich experience from the moment they get in line until they finally step off the ride and exit through the gift shop. As a result, roller coaster designers work closely with artists, musicians, and storytellers who can provide the sights and sounds that turn a two-minute ride into a memory passengers will never forget.

STORY TIME

Theme park rides often tell a story to passengers. Often, these rides are based on movies, TV shows, or comic books. This is especially common at theme parks such as Disneyland or Universal Studios, where the owners have plenty of popular characters they can use to promote their rides. Even while passengers wait in line, the rides transport them into new worlds.

Some of these rides might have video presentations or audio recordings to help explain the story being told. For example, a *Harry Potter*–themed ride at Islands of Adventure in Orlando replicates the

Space Mountain in Disneyland features an elaborate sci-fi setting to keep riders interested as they wait in line for the coaster.

famous scene from the movies where Harry learns to ride a winged creature called a Hippogriff. As passengers wait in line, they can hear the character Hagrid explaining how to ride a Hippogriff.

GOOD LOOKS

Everything from the colors and shapes of the coaster to the visuals displayed alongside lines of waiting passengers can add to the experience of a thrill ride. Colors for tracks and trains are chosen carefully to catch the eyes of park guests and potential guests who might pass by the park.

LISTEN TO THE MUSIC

Some coasters are also accompanied by music designed to get passengers pumped for the ride. The Hollywood Rip Ride Rockit at Universal Studios Orlando even allows each rider to select which song he or she wants to hear while riding the coaster. Speakers in the coaster seats can play different music for each passenger.

Sometimes theme parks pay established artists to play their songs on rides. In other situations, they might hire composers to create original music especially for each ride. ✴

WILD EAGLE AT DOLLYWOOD IN TENNESSEE

Drafters usually create architectural drawings with the help of computer software.

DRAWING DESIGNS

Once engineers have settled on their plans for a ride, they create the technical drawings that will be used as a guide for the actual construction process. The creation of these drawings is known as drafting. Some engineers handle their own drafting, while others work with drafting specialists.

Drafting can be done by hand, but it is more often accomplished using computer-aided design (CAD) software. Drafters use CAD programs to create computer-generated plans for new coaster designs. These drawings contain all the information a construction team needs to assemble a ride from the ground up.

A FOOT IN THE DOOR

Roller coaster design is a tough field to break into. It is a difficult job that requires a lot of specialized knowledge, and there are a limited number of coaster companies in the world. One way budding coaster designers get their start is by working as interns for experienced designers. Interns play an important role in the coaster creation process. They assist the designers with simple tasks to help them save time and effort for the more difficult parts of their jobs. In return, interns get firsthand experience in designing roller coasters and make connections with important people in the field. Most interns are college students or recent graduates. If an intern does an especially good job, he or she might be hired as a full-fledged employee.

Interns get an opportunity to learn on the job and meet people in the industry in exchange for helping out with basic tasks.

Huge crowds of thrill seekers line up to be among the first to ride new coasters.

4

COASTER CREATION

t's not easy to build a roller coaster. Even the simplest ride requires an incredible amount of planning and effort to bring it from an idea to a reality. Roller coasters also take a lot of time and money to build. Because they are such large undertakings, only about 20 to 30 major new rides are built around the world each year, in addition to a variety of smaller projects. As a result, a roller coaster company might only work on one or two projects a year. Each new coaster is treated with the utmost care and attention, and a new project can never be rushed out the door. Even a quickly built coaster can take up to nine months to plan and build.

FASTER AND FASTER

2001	2003	2005	2010
Reaching speeds of nearly 107 miles per hour (172 kph), Dodonpa in Japan becomes the world's fastest coaster.	Top Thrill Dragster takes the speed crown, topping out at 120 miles per hour (193 kph).	Kingda Ka breaks roller coaster speed records by reaching 128 miles per hour (206 kph).	At 149 miles per hour (240 kph), Formula Rossa races faster than any previous coaster.

FIRST STEPS

The process of designing and building a coaster begins when a theme park decides it is ready to add a new ride to its roster. The park might need to compete with its rivals' newer, more advanced coasters. It might also simply want to draw in a new kind of audience. Park officials share these ideas with the design team and begin working together to develop a more solid plan.

The degree of involvement that a park has with a coaster's design varies greatly. Sometimes park officials know exactly what they want to build and what space is available. Other times a park sets a budget and gives the designers freedom to do what they can with a certain amount of money. Park officials might also provide the height or length of the ride they want and allow the designers to fill in the rest of the details.

A single new coaster can draw massive crowds into a theme park.

METAL RAILS HELP MANAGE LARGE
CROWDS INTO ORGANIZED LINES

Scale models can help make it easier for people to visualize what a completed coaster will look like.

BRAINSTORMING

The design team must take the park owners' requests into account as they brainstorm ideas for the new ride. They must also consider practical matters. For example, they will only have a certain amount of space to build the ride, and that space will be in a certain shape. The **topography** of the park also plays a big part in the design of the ride. Ground is rarely flat, so coaster designers plan their designs around hills, valleys, and other land features.

Designers also consider how the ride will fit in with the rest of the park's attractions. For example, the direction a lift hill faces might be determined based on what view it will offer riders when they reach the top.

With these factors in mind, the designers begin thinking of shapes and elements that might not have been tried before. They use computer software to create 3D models of their ideas. These 3D models are often animated to show what the completed coaster will look like as it hurtles along the tracks.

WHERE THE MAGIC HAPPENS

BOLLIGER & MABILLARD

Of all the roller coaster companies in the world, Bolliger & Mabillard (B&M) stands out as one of the greatest. Located in Monthey, Switzerland, the company was formed in 1988. Since then, B&M has created dozens of roller coasters and made a name for itself as the premier designer of unique and groundbreaking rides.

OUT ON THEIR OWN

During the 1970s and 1980s, Walter Bolliger and Claude Mabillard worked as engineers for Giovanola Freres, a large

Swiss company that designed roller coasters for such major coaster companies as Intamin. They left to form their own engineering company in 1988, and two years later they built B&M's first coaster. Iron Wolf, a stand-up coaster at Six Flags Great America in Illinois, was the tallest and fastest stand-up coaster in the world when it opened. Its success put B&M on the map, and B&M has since grown to become a firm of 37 people.

Iron Wolf operated from 1990 until 2011.

Goliath, a B&M coaster at Six Flags Over Georgia, reaches speeds of 70 miles per hour (113 kph).

IDEAS AND INNOVATIONS

B&M has been behind many of the biggest changes in coaster technology since its founding. In 1992, Batman: The Ride introduced the world to inverted coasters. Oblivion, which opened in 1998 at England's Alton Towers, was the first coaster to include a full 90-degree vertical drop. B&M introduced floorless coasters, which allow passengers to sit with their legs dangling in front of them, with 1999's Medusa. One of the company's most recent innovations is the wing coaster. In a wing coaster, riders sit alongside the track instead of on top of it or below it.

GOING GIGA

In 2012, B&M unleashed its very first giga coaster. The 306-foot (93 m) Leviathan is located at Canada's Wonderland, in Ontario. It is the seventh-tallest and eighth-fastest coaster in the world. ✷

Roller coaster designers sometimes modify their plans even after construction has begun.

STAYING ON TRACK

Once the coaster's design has been approved by the park owners, the team can begin planning the construction process. Theme parks rely on new rides to open on schedule to help them start making back the money they have spent creating and promoting the attraction. As a result, roller coaster companies are always under pressure to meet deadlines and follow budgets.

To help make sure they can meet these goals, they outline a schedule for the construction. They must account for how long it will take to get certain building materials. They must also plan for the time they will need to spend testing the ride.

A RIDE'S RECIPE

Choosing the right building materials is an important part of building any large structure. Engineers must ensure that the materials they use will be sturdy and hold up over time.

At the same time, the designers must keep their budget in mind. Some materials can be much more expensive than others. If one type of wood is very expensive, the team might look for an option that works just as well but costs less.

Finally, the team must take the look of the coaster into account. If the final product does not look fun or exciting, park visitors might not want to ride it. Choosing the right shapes and colors for materials is a big part of getting the right look for a ride.

Artists create images like this one of Kingda Ka to show what a final coaster will look like, from its shape to its color.

Once the plans are finalized, the actual construction process can begin.

FINALIZING THE PLANS

Before construction begins, the designers must create final drawings to work from. They work with drafters to draw up the plans and then go over them carefully one last time to make sure they didn't make any mistakes. These plans contain all of the measurements and material specifications for each piece that will go into the coaster's construction. They also contain instructions for building the more complex parts of the project. Engineers review the drafters' work and make any necessary last-minute tweaks, and then the final plans are prepared.

FROM THE BOTTOM TO THE TOP

After all of that preparation, it finally comes time to break ground and begin building the coaster. The construction site is blocked off to prevent guests from wandering in, and the construction crew begins arriving with cranes, loaders, and other heavy equipment. The designers also make visits to the site to check in on the construction process. Because a roller coaster company's clients come from all over the world, this often means they must travel great distances.

The construction team begins by digging a hole for the concrete foundation that will anchor the coaster's main supports to the ground. They use cranes to move large, heavy pieces into place and then bolt them together. Little by little, the structure begins to look like a coaster.

Coaster construction crews must climb high above the ground to assemble the pieces of a new ride.

LASTING CONTRIBUTIONS

Side-friction and underfriction wheels, also known as side wheels and upstop wheels, are an important safety feature on modern coasters.

WONDROUS WHEELS

A roller coaster train car originally had one set of wheels that rode on the top of the rails and a second wheel, called a side-friction wheel, that skidded along the sides of the rails. Beneath the rails was a plate or bar that helped keep the coaster trains from popping off of the tracks. However, as more rides began including moments of airtime, these plates or bars would rub against the bottom of the track, slowing the coaster cars down. In 1919, the legendary coaster designer John Miller solved this dilemma by adding a third set of wheels that rolled beneath the rails. He called these wheels the underfriction wheels. Miller's three-part wheel assembly kept a car locked onto the rails without slowing it down as much.

EXTREMELY SAFE

The increase in safety also led to another improvement in coaster technology. With less chance of a coaster popping off the rails, designers were able to create more extreme rides. Designers, Miller included, trusted the new wheels to keep people safe on coasters with steeper hills, sharper turns, and higher speeds.

Without modern safety features, many of today's twisting, turning coasters would be impossible.

Underfriction wheels allow coaster trains to hang from the tracks without falling.

STAYING POWER

Underfriction wheels continue to keep coaster cars locked onto their tracks even today. Without Miller's ingenious innovation, many of today's rides would be impossible. Though the underfriction wheel is a simple idea, it has had a big effect! ✹

Designers sometimes test stretches of track as a coaster is constructed.

TESTING TIME

As the coaster draws nearer to completion, the engineers begin testing it to make sure everything functions correctly and the ride is safe. During construction, they test the various mechanical and electronic systems on the coaster individually to make sure they work like they are supposed to.

Once the coaster is close to finished, the engineers test it out by putting weights in the seats. These weights are sometimes human-shaped dummies. Other times, they are simply bags of corn or lead. During the test runs, designers measure the force exerted on the coasters and tracks to ensure that it matches their planned design. They also run the coaster several times to make sure that all computer systems are functioning properly. These first tests do not use human riders because it could be extremely dangerous if something goes wrong. Once the engineers have determined that the ride is safe, they can ride it themselves to make sure it is fun and comfortable.

ALMOST READY

The park builds anticipation for its new ride by advertising the new attraction. It might hold special previews of the ride for members of the press, friends of the park owners, or other lucky park guests. It might also use social networks such as Twitter and Facebook to share photos and videos of the upcoming coaster. Soon, word begins to spread among coaster fans. Anticipation builds as they look forward to trying the new ride.

Finally, it comes time for the grand opening of the new coaster. Huge lines form, and the people leaving the ride can't stop smiling. It's a huge hit! Satisfied with their work, the designers head back to the office. Even though they just finished a major project, they are already planning new twists, turns, and loops.

HUMAN-SHAPED DUMMIES RECORD COASTER DATA

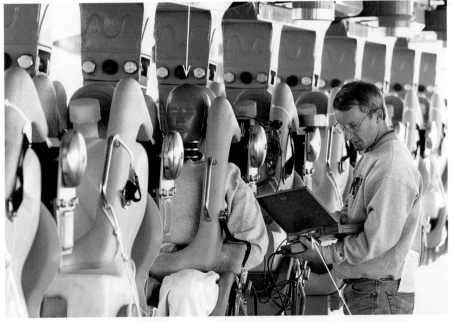

Some crash dummies are equipped with devices that measure the speed and forces placed on riders of a coaster.

DESIGNERS CONNECT COMPUTERS TO DUMMIES TO RETRIEVE DATA

THE FUTURE

Roller coasters just keep getting bigger, faster, and more fun as engineers find creative new ways to improve on the thrills people have been enjoying for hundreds of years. Roller coasters have a long history. But the ride's future promises to go on for even longer. Engineers are said to be at work already on creating a coaster that is more than 500 feet (152 m) tall. The sky may really be the limit for roller coasters.

Passengers travel alongside the tracks as they zoom through the loops, rolls, and corkscrews of Dollywood's Wild Eagle coaster.

NEW WAYS TO RIDE

Roller coaster designers are increasingly looking toward the coaster trains themselves for new ways to make rides stand out. They are trying out all kinds of new ways to sit, stand, and hang from coaster tracks. The potential seating options are almost endless. On Wild Eagle, at Dollywood in Pigeon Forge, Tennessee, riders sit in seats that run alongside the coaster's track.

Some designers are also working with designs that allow coaster cars to spin in different directions as they move along the tracks. Some future coasters might even be able to spin both vertically and horizontally.

READY TO LAUNCH

Coaster designers are also working with new methods of coaster propulsion. Cheetah Hunt at Busch Gardens in Tampa, Florida, uses powerful **electromagnets** to speed the coasters along the tracks. This system allows the coaster to suddenly accelerate at three points along the ride, giving riders an unexpected burst of speed. Such systems might only be the beginning of what coaster designers can accomplish with electromagnets in the future. ✷

Cheetah Hunt at Busch Gardens is just one example of the new and exciting possibilities of electromagnetic coasters.

CAREER STATS

CIVIL ENGINEERS

MEDIAN ANNUAL SALARY (2010): $77,560

NUMBER OF JOBS (2010): 262,800

PROJECTED JOB GROWTH: 19%, average growth

PROJECTED INCREASE IN JOBS 2010–2020: 51,100

REQUIRED EDUCATION: Bachelor's degree

LICENSE/CERTIFICATION: State license, available after four years of experience; test requirements vary by state

MECHANICAL ENGINEERS

MEDIAN ANNUAL SALARY (2010): $78,160

NUMBER OF JOBS (2010): 243,200

PROJECTED JOB GROWTH: 9%, slower than average

PROJECTED INCREASE IN JOBS 2010–2020: 21,300

REQUIRED EDUCATION: Bachelor's degree

LICENSE/CERTIFICATION: State license, available after four years of experience; test requirements vary by state

DRAFTERS

MEDIAN ANNUAL SALARY (2010): $47,880

NUMBER OF JOBS (2010): 205,100

PROJECTED JOB GROWTH: 6%, slower than average

PROJECTED INCREASE IN JOBS 2010–2020: 11,400

REQUIRED EDUCATION: Associate's degree

LICENSE/CERTIFICATION: None

Figures reported by the United States Bureau of Labor Statistics

RESOURCES

BOOKS

Bodden, Valerie. *Roller Coasters*. Mankato, MN: Creative Education, 2012.

Koll, Hilary, Steve Mills, and Korey T. Kiepert. *Using Math to Design a Roller Coaster*. Pleasantville, NY: Gareth Stevens, 2007.

Mitchell, Susan K. *The Biggest Thrill Rides*. Pleasantville, NY: Gareth Stevens, 2008.

Newton, Joan. *Gravity in Action: Roller Coasters!* New York: PowerKids, 2009.

Rau, Dana Meachen. *Roller Coasters*. Pelham, NY: Benchmark, 2011.

Schaefer, Adam R. *Roller Coasters*. North Mankato, MN: Edge Books, 2005.

Sohn, Emily, and Hansen, Anya. *Models and Designs: It's a Roller Coaster Ride!* Chicago: Norwood House, 2011.

Tocci, Salvatore. *Experiments with Gravity*. New York: Children's Press, 2002.

FACTS FOR NOW

Visit this Scholastic Web site
for more information on roller coasters:
www.factsfornow.scholastic.com
Enter the keywords **Roller Coasters**

GLOSSARY

accelerate (ik-SEL-uh-rate) to move faster and faster

airtime (AIR-time) moments on a roller coaster ride where riders feel as if their bodies are weightless

diesel (DEE-zuhl) a fuel used in diesel engines that is heavier than gasoline

electromagnets (i-LEK-troh-mag-nits) magnets that are formed when electricity flows through coils of wire

engineers (en-juh-NEERZ) people who are specially trained to design and build machines or large structures such as bridges and roads

friction (FRIK-shuhn) the force that slows down objects when they rub against each other

hydraulic (hye-DRAW-lik) powered by fluid pressure

inversion (in-VUR-zhuhn) a part of a roller coaster track in which riders are turned upside down

patents (PAT-uhnts) legal documents giving the inventor of an item the sole rights to manufacture or sell it

pneumatic (noo-MAT-ik) powered by compressed air

terrain (tuh-RAYN) an area of land

topography (tuh-PAH-gruh-fee) the detailed description of the physical features of an area, including hills, valleys, mountains, plains, and rivers

vertical (VUR-ti-kuhl) upright, or straight up and down

INDEX

Page numbers in *italics* indicate illustrations.

INDEX (CONTINUED)

ABOUT THE AUTHOR

KEVIN CUNNINGHAM graduated from the University of Illinois at Urbana. He is the author of more than 60 books on history, health, disasters, and other topics. He lives near Chicago, Illinois.